D1423367

Who were the Vikings?

Jane Chisholm & Struan Reid

Illustrated by David Cuzik

Designed by Vicki Groombridge

Edited by Phil Roxbee Cox
History consultant: Dr. Anne Millard

CONTENTS

Usborne Quicklinks

For links to websites where you can find out lots more about the
Vikings and how they lived, go to the Usborne Quicklinks website at
www.usborne.com/quicklinks and type in the keywords **starting vikings**.
Please follow the internet safety guidelines displayed at the Usborne Quicklinks website.

Who were the Vikings?

People who lived in Scandinavia (Sweden, Norway and Denmark) over 1,300 years ago. They were fierce warriors and seafarers who attacked towns and villages all over Europe. The Vikings were hated and feared by their victims, which isn't at all surprising.

Eric the Red, a Viking explorer, settled in Greenland after being expelled from Norway and Iceland.

ICELAND

This is a statue of Leif Ericsson, a Norwegian Viking who was probably the first European to set foot in America.

In 1066, England was conquered by Normans, who were descended from Vikings.

Why didn't they just stay at home?

The number of people grew quickly, and there wasn't enough good land for everyone to have their own farm. Usually the eldest sons got all the land. Many raiders were landless younger sons who wanted to get rich quick.

The city of Dublin was founded by Vikings.

IRELAND

Dublin

ATLANTIC OCEAN

SCOTLAND

NORWAY

SWEDEN

ENGLAND

DENMARK

Irish treasure was looted by the Vikings.

The arrows show some of the places the Vikings went.

FRANCE

Were they only savage warriors?

No. Many Vikings were farmers, craftspeople and traders. They were also great adventurers and explorers. Some went as far as the Middle East and across the Atlantic Ocean to America.

Carved head of a Viking god

SPAIN

Normandy, in France, is named after Vikings (called Northmen, or Normans) who settled there.

ITALY

Silver cup

MEDITERRANEAN SEA

A Viking warrior carved from reindeer antler

2

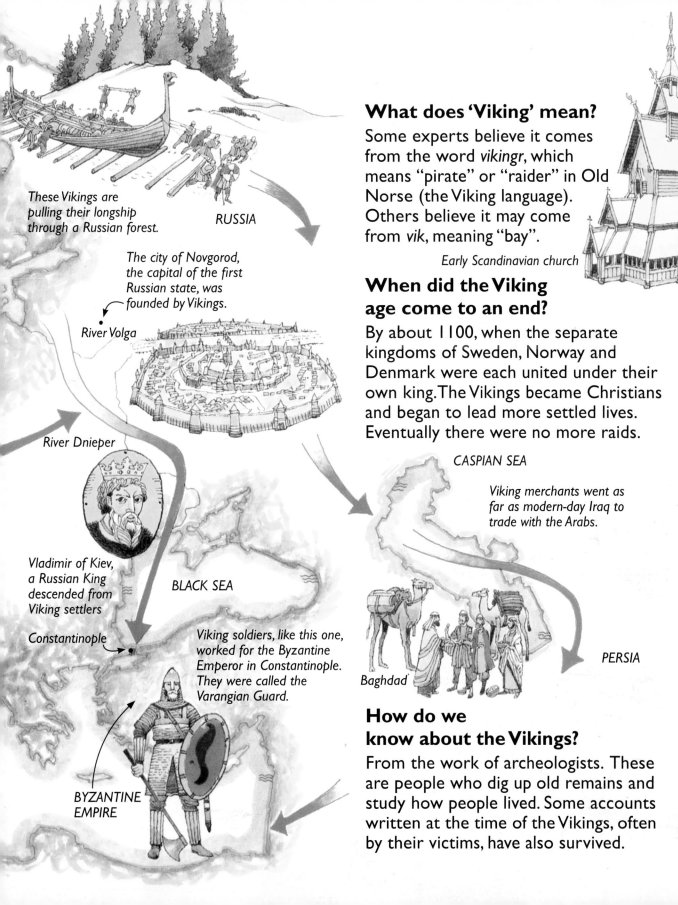

These Vikings are pulling their longship through a Russian forest.

RUSSIA

The city of Novgorod, the capital of the first Russian state, was founded by Vikings.

River Volga

River Dnieper

Vladimir of Kiev, a Russian King descended from Viking settlers

Constantinople

BLACK SEA

Viking soldiers, like this one, worked for the Byzantine Emperor in Constantinople. They were called the Varangian Guard.

BYZANTINE EMPIRE

What does 'Viking' mean?

Some experts believe it comes from the word *vikingr*, which means "pirate" or "raider" in Old Norse (the Viking language). Others believe it may come from *vik*, meaning "bay".

Early Scandinavian church

When did the Viking age come to an end?

By about 1100, when the separate kingdoms of Sweden, Norway and Denmark were each united under their own king. The Vikings became Christians and began to lead more settled lives. Eventually there were no more raids.

CASPIAN SEA

Viking merchants went as far as modern-day Iraq to trade with the Arabs.

Baghdad

PERSIA

How do we know about the Vikings?

From the work of archeologists. These are people who dig up old remains and study how people lived. Some accounts written at the time of the Vikings, often by their victims, have also survived.

3

People often imagine Vikings as tall and fierce-looking, with long red beards and helmets with wings or horns on them. In fact, some Vikings may have been quite small, and their helmets definitely didn't have horns.

What clothes did they wear?

Really warm ones. It was pretty cold most of the time. The women wore long dresses and the men wore trousers and tunics. These were usually made of wool or linen. They had thick cloaks of wool or fur.

A Viking frightening his enemies

Did they really have big red beards?

Only the ones with red hair. And none of the women and children. Viking men did grow beards, probably to keep warm, look fierce and avoid shaving. But some of them would have had fair or even dark hair.

Loom

Weights

Sword arm free in case of emergencies

Leather skullcap

Expensive tunic trimmed with Chinese silk

Cloak pinned on one shoulder

Headscarf

Tunic dress

Viking chief

This merchant bought his fur hat and baggy trousers in Russia.

Leather shoes

Where did they get their clothes?

The women made them at home. First they dyed wool and linen threads (from a plant called flax) with dyes made from plants and rocks. Then they wove the threads on a loom, then sewed them together into clothes.

Were there Viking hairdressers?

No, but Vikings took great care over how they looked. Women wore their long hair tied back or in braids. The men often had long hair too, and sometimes braided their beards. This stopped the beards from blowing into their faces in the wind.

Some Viking hairstyles

This man is very pleased with his beard.

Do you know what these are?

Viking women didn't carry handbags. They hung the things they needed on a chain hanging from a brooch. Can you guess what these three items are? (Find out on page 32.)

Did they paint their faces?

Yes, and not just the women. According to one visiting Arab trader, the men painted black powder called kohl around their eyes – not to look pretty, but to appear even more frightening to their enemies.

Did they wear jewels?

Plenty of them. Both men and women wore rings and bracelets. Because they didn't use buttons, they usually kept their clothes in place with belts and brooches.

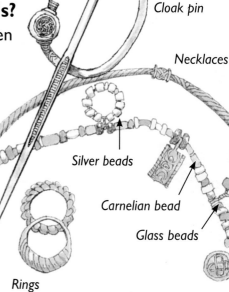

Cloak pin

Necklaces

Silver beads

Carnelian bead

Glass beads

Rings

Brooch

Earrings

Bracelet

5

What was a Viking family like?

Very big and, if you were lucky, friendly too. Children, parents, grandparents, aunts, uncles and cousins all lived together in the same village – sometimes even in the same house. They all helped each other. Being loyal to the family was very important.

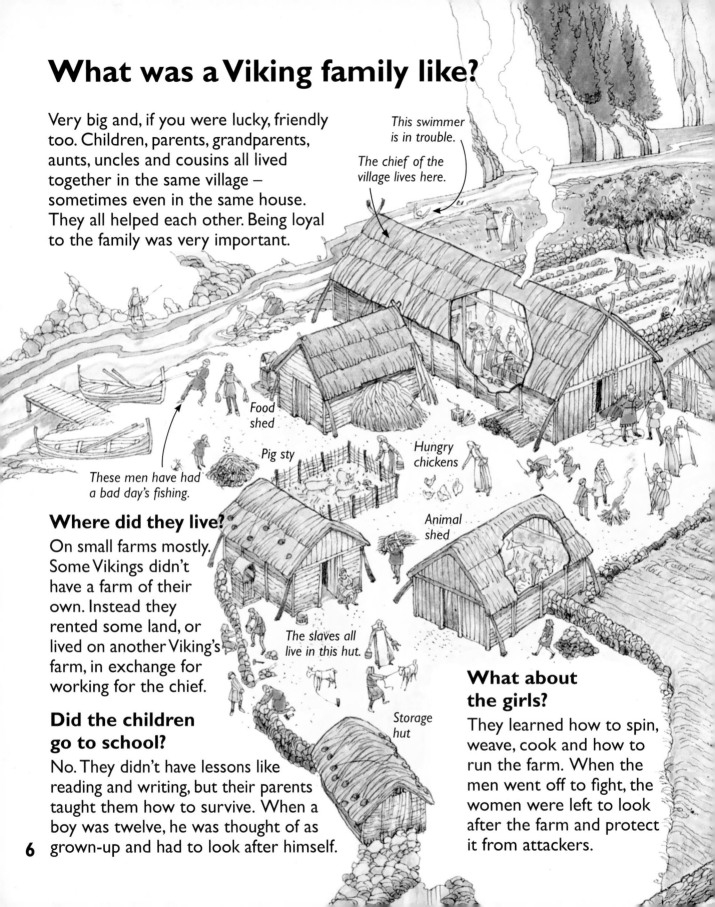

This swimmer is in trouble.

The chief of the village lives here.

These men have had a bad day's fishing.

Food shed

Pig sty

Hungry chickens

Animal shed

The slaves all live in this hut.

Storage hut

Where did they live?
On small farms mostly. Some Vikings didn't have a farm of their own. Instead they rented some land, or lived on another Viking's farm, in exchange for working for the chief.

Did the children go to school?
No. They didn't have lessons like reading and writing, but their parents taught them how to survive. When a boy was twelve, he was thought of as grown-up and had to look after himself.

What about the girls?
They learned how to spin, weave, cook and how to run the farm. When the men went off to fight, the women were left to look after the farm and protect it from attackers.

6

Building a
new warship

Spear-throwing

Hungry
ducks

These men
are training
for battle.

Sowing seeds

Back from a good day's hunting

What did they grow?

Whatever they could.
This included cereals
like oats, barley, wheat
and rye, and vegetables
such as cabbages, onions,
beans and peas, but no
potatoes. They hadn't
been discovered yet.

What animals
did they keep?

The usual ones: pigs, sheep,
goats, cattle, chickens,
ducks and geese.

*Blacksmith's workshop, where the
blacksmith makes tools and weapons
from iron. It's hot and smoky here.*

*Chunks of iron ore are burned
with charcoal in these clay ovens.
The fire melts them into iron.*

Did they go hunting and fishing?

Yes, when they weren't farming or raiding.
They hunted birds and large animals, such
as elk, deer, wild boar (pig) and sometimes
bear. They also went fishing, and hunted
large sea animals such as walruses, seals,
and even whales.

7

What were Viking houses like?

Long, usually. In fact, so long that they were called 'longhouses'. A longhouse was usually just one big room, where everyone ate, slept, worked and relaxed together. Only the chief and his wife sometimes had a room to themselves.

What were the houses made of?

Wood, mostly. The frame was built of strong wooden posts. The walls were made of logs, or woven wooden canes, plastered with mud to make them thicker and stronger. The roof was thatched with reeds or straw. There were no windows.

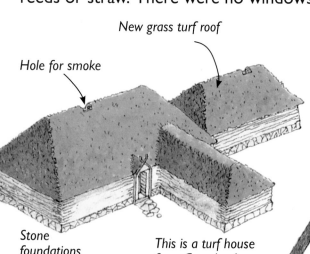

Hole for smoke

New grass turf roof

Stone foundations

This is a turf house from Greenland.

Were all the houses made like this?

No. In some places, such as Greenland, there weren't enough trees to make wooden houses. The Vikings built rather different houses there out of stone and turf (squares of grass and mud cut out of the ground). Thick turf helped keep the icy wind out.

Why didn't they have windows?

Because they would have let the cold in. This made it very dark inside. The only light came from the fire and from small clay lamps burning oil.

Woven wall-hanging

This man is repairing a broken sword.

Loom for weaving

This is a Viking longhouse. The artist has cut away part of the roof so you can see inside.

Food is cooked over the fire in the middle.

More wood for the fire

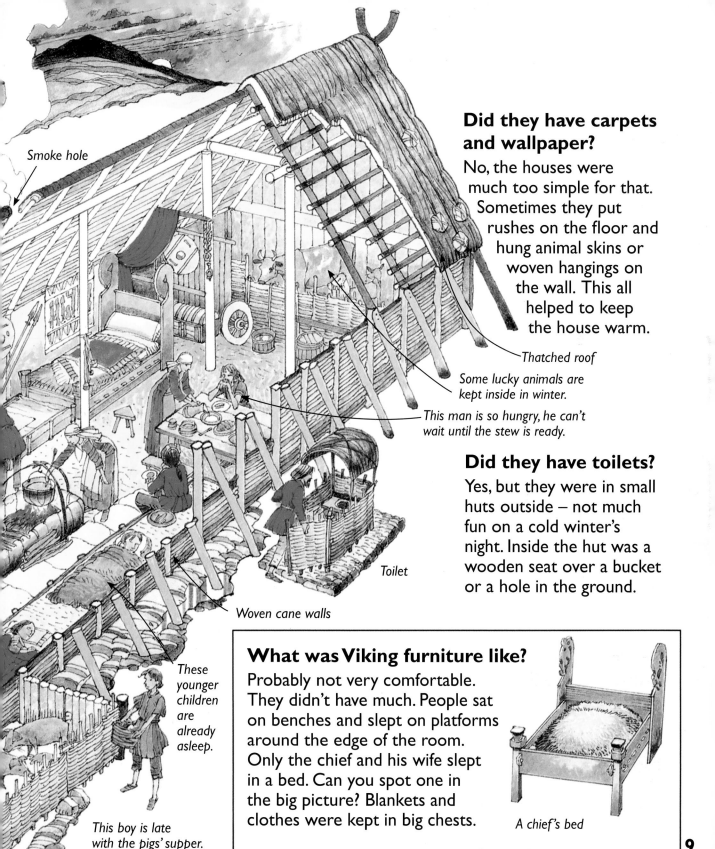

Smoke hole

Did they have carpets and wallpaper?

No, the houses were much too simple for that. Sometimes they put rushes on the floor and hung animal skins or woven hangings on the wall. This all helped to keep the house warm.

Thatched roof

Some lucky animals are kept inside in winter.

This man is so hungry, he can't wait until the stew is ready.

Did they have toilets?

Yes, but they were in small huts outside – not much fun on a cold winter's night. Inside the hut was a wooden seat over a bucket or a hole in the ground.

Toilet

Woven cane walls

These younger children are already asleep.

This boy is late with the pigs' supper.

What was Viking furniture like?

Probably not very comfortable. They didn't have much. People sat on benches and slept on platforms around the edge of the room. Only the chief and his wife slept in a bed. Can you spot one in the big picture? Blankets and clothes were kept in big chests.

A chief's bed

Did the Vikings believe in God?

They believed in many different gods and goddesses, who lived in a place called Asgard. The only way to reach Asgard was across a rainbow bridge called Bifrost. Vikings believed that their own world, called Midgard, was in the middle of a deep sea full of monsters.

Who was the most important god?

Odin. He was powerful and dangerous, as well as mysterious and wise. Odin could change into any bird or animal. Everyone was afraid of him.

Did they believe in the Devil?

No, but they believed in a naughty god called Loki. When things went wrong, people often blamed Loki. They also believed in wicked giants, dwarfs and dark elves.

Who were the giants and dwarfs?

The giants were evil creatures who often caused trouble. They lived in mountains across the sea from Midgard. The dwarfs were ugly and greedy, but very good at making things out of gold.

Which god did people like best?

Thor. He was big and jolly, with a bushy red beard and a booming laugh. People thought that thunder and lightning came from Thor riding his chariot across the skies.

Odin

Thor's magic hammer, Mjollnir

Sleipnir, Odin's eight-legged horse

Thor

Goats pulling Thor's chariot

Dwarfs

Loki

Giant

All these worlds are held together by the roots of a magic tree called Yggdrasil.

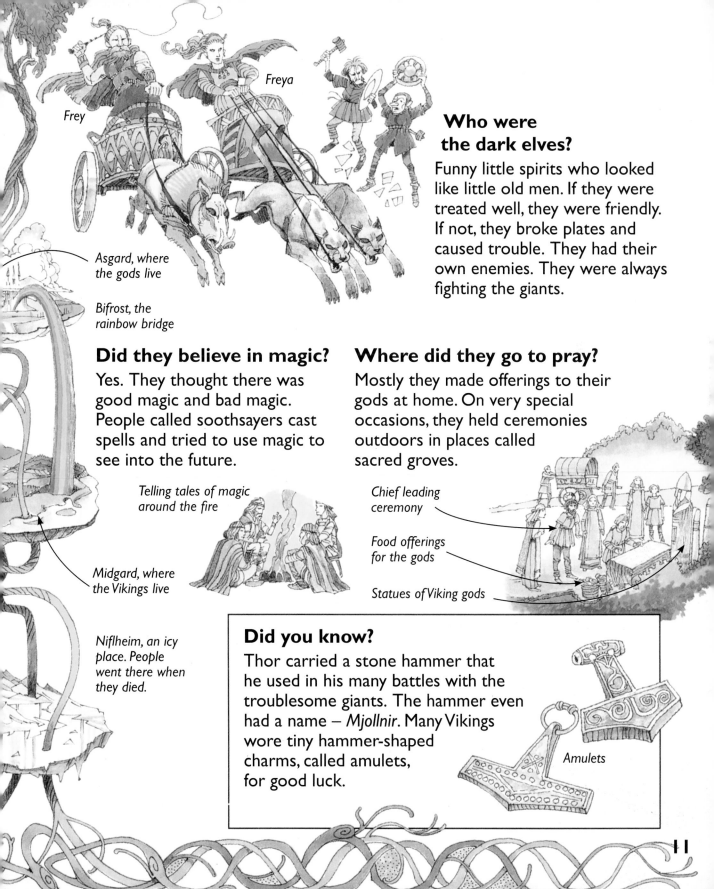

Freya

Frey

Asgard, where
the gods live

Bifrost, the
rainbow bridge

Midgard, where
the Vikings live

Niflheim, an icy
place. People
went there when
they died.

Who were the dark elves?

Funny little spirits who looked like little old men. If they were treated well, they were friendly. If not, they broke plates and caused trouble. They had their own enemies. They were always fighting the giants.

Did they believe in magic?

Yes. They thought there was good magic and bad magic. People called soothsayers cast spells and tried to use magic to see into the future.

Telling tales of magic
around the fire

Where did they go to pray?

Mostly they made offerings to their gods at home. On very special occasions, they held ceremonies outdoors in places called sacred groves.

Chief leading
ceremony

Food offerings
for the gods

Statues of Viking gods

Did you know?

Thor carried a stone hammer that he used in his many battles with the troublesome giants. The hammer even had a name – *Mjollnir*. Many Vikings wore tiny hammer-shaped charms, called amulets, for good luck.

Amulets

What happened if they were ill?

They were usually looked after at home. If a warrior was wounded in battle, another warrior might help dress and bandage his wounds.

Didn't they have doctors?

No, but some people knew all about making medicines from herbs and mending broken bones. Magic spells were expected to play a big part too.

This Viking chief has been wounded in battle. He's really getting too old for fighting.

The women do most of the work, including brewing herbs to make potions.

The chief's brother is bandaging his arm. He has been wounded several times himself.

Medicine chest

Faithful hounds

Hot work

This boy is about to get into trouble.

This is the chief's sister. She looks very worried.

Her son looks more interested in his new puppy.

This warrior broke his sword and shield in battle.

What happened if the person died?

That depended on how important they were. Most people were just buried in a hole in the ground. Some warriors were burned on a pile of wood, called a pyre.

Food and drink

The body of a great chief or warrior was often buried in a ship, together with treasure and weapons. People thought it would sail off to Valhalla, guided by Valkyries.

12

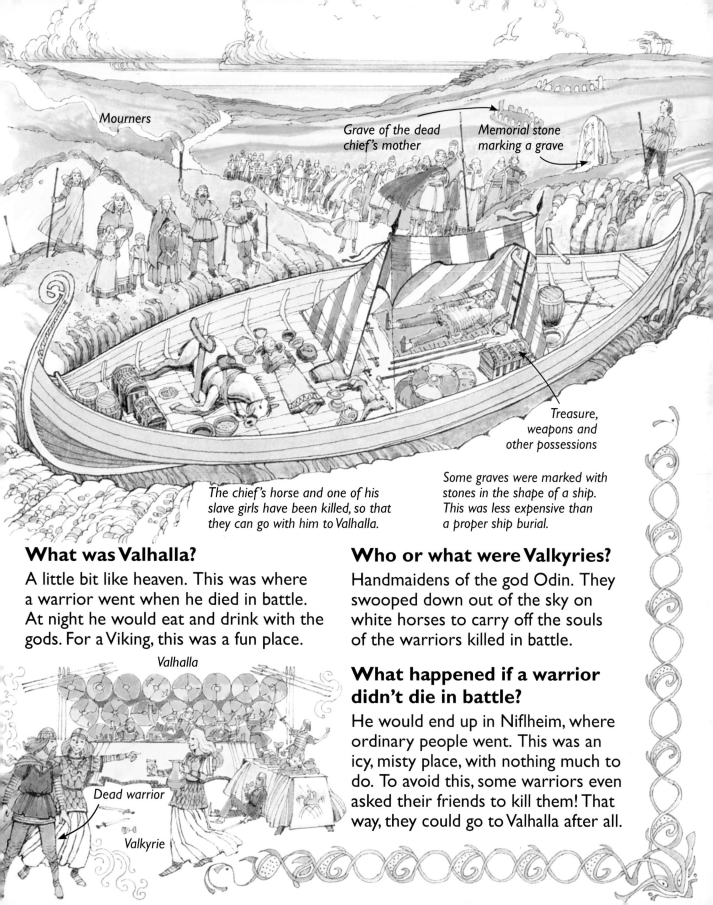

Mourners

Grave of the dead chief's mother

Memorial stone marking a grave

Treasure, weapons and other possessions

The chief's horse and one of his slave girls have been killed, so that they can go with him to Valhalla.

Some graves were marked with stones in the shape of a ship. This was less expensive than a proper ship burial.

What was Valhalla?

A little bit like heaven. This was where a warrior went when he died in battle. At night he would eat and drink with the gods. For a Viking, this was a fun place.

Valhalla

Dead warrior

Valkyrie

Who or what were Valkyries?

Handmaidens of the god Odin. They swooped down out of the sky on white horses to carry off the souls of the warriors killed in battle.

What happened if a warrior didn't die in battle?

He would end up in Niflheim, where ordinary people went. This was an icy, misty place, with nothing much to do. To avoid this, some warriors even asked their friends to kill them! That way, they could go to Valhalla after all.

What was Viking food like?

Pretty boring, probably. They could only eat what they could grow and hunt. The climate wasn't good enough for them to grow a great variety of food, and hunting was quite difficult in winter.

Drinking horn (the wrong way up)

Wooden bucket

Viking jugs and bowls

How do we know what they ate?

Because archeologists have found seeds and animal and fish bones in Viking graves.

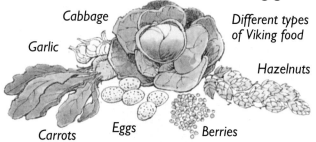

Cabbage

Garlic

Different types of Viking food

Hazelnuts

Carrots

Eggs

Berries

How did they manage in winter?

By eating meat and fish that had been packed in salt to preserve it. But this didn't help to make it taste nice.

Hunting in several feet of snow wouldn't have been much fun.

Did they have parties?

Yes, on special occasions. After an enormous meal, musicians played harps and pipes and a professional poet, called a skald, recited poems – usually about the chief's daring deeds!

A little arm-wrestling

They eat with their fingers, knives and spoons. They don't have forks.

Yet another fight

They are drinking ale (a kind of beer) or mead (a drink made from apples and honey).

This dog is hoping for a goose for supper.

How did they cook the food?

Food could be grilled or spit-roasted over a fire, or baked in a hole in the ground packed with hot stones. Boiling or stewing was done by hanging a pot over the fire from a hook on the ceiling.

What was their music like?

Mostly harp or pipe music. We can only guess what it sounded like. Al-Tartushi, an Arab merchant, said the noise of Vikings singing was worse than howling dogs!

Did they drink a lot?

Yes, quite often. Some Viking raiders waited for people to get drunk before they attacked them. Then they couldn't defend themselves.

An enthusiastic toast

A drinking horn the right way up

This man has a headache.

A skald reciting a poem

Harpist harping

Piper piping

A thirsty drinker

Make Viking wild berry juice

Mash raspberries, blackberries or strawberries in a strainer over a bowl to get the juice out. Then add water (about the same amount), and honey to taste.

What did the Vikings do for fun?

All sorts of things. When they weren't fighting, farming, hunting or housekeeping, they were enjoying themselves. They didn't have organized sports as we do, but if they got together for a special occasion, they often challenged each other to fights and competitions.

What sorts of competitions did they have?

Anything they were good at. Here are some of the different sports they played.

A stubborn pig

Wrestling

Swordfights could be quite dangerous, especially after a banquet when people had had a lot to drink.

The wrestler who lands on the stone is the loser.

This man finds weight-lifting very easy →

The referee is here to make sure nobody cheats.

Chasing chickens

This man isn't as strong as he thought he was.

A jump about to end in a bump

Did they have time off?

No, but they did celebrate three big religious festivals every year – at the beginning of summer, at harvest time and in the middle of winter. At each one, there were huge parties that went on for days.

Smoked fish

Two people are crazy enough to swim in the icy water. Can you spot them?

More food for the feast

Guests arriving

Didn't they get bored in winter?

Probably not, because the days were short and there was lots to do. They played board games and told endless stories, called sagas. There was a popular game called _hnefatfl_, which may have been something like chess. The exact rules have never been found.

These two have heard the story before. They'd rather play a game.

This storyteller is very popular.

What were the sagas about?

Gods, heroes, battles, great adventures, distant lands and strange people. Sagas were passed down through the family from the oldest to the youngest. Some were so long that it took days to tell them.

Which saga did they like best?

Probably one with Thor in it. For a god, he wasn't very clever and kept on ending up in trouble. The ways he managed to escape were very exciting. There is a story about Thor on the next page.

Did you know?

Viking traders may have watched chess games in the Middle East. They probably liked the game so much they brought the idea back with them. Then they would have made their own pieces and taught a version to their friends at home.

Viking game pieces

17

There's more on the next page...

The night in the forest

Thor was the eldest son of Odin, king of the gods. He used his muscles when others would have used their wits. Thor loved a good battle or a trial of strength. In search of adventure, Thor decided to travel to Utgard, home of the giants. The giants were sworn enemies of the gods.

After a long day's travel, Thor and his fellow adventurers found themselves deep in the heart of a forest. In the gloomy twilight, they spotted the entrance to a strange building at the foot of a small mountain. There was no door, just an enormous opening like the mouth of a cave.

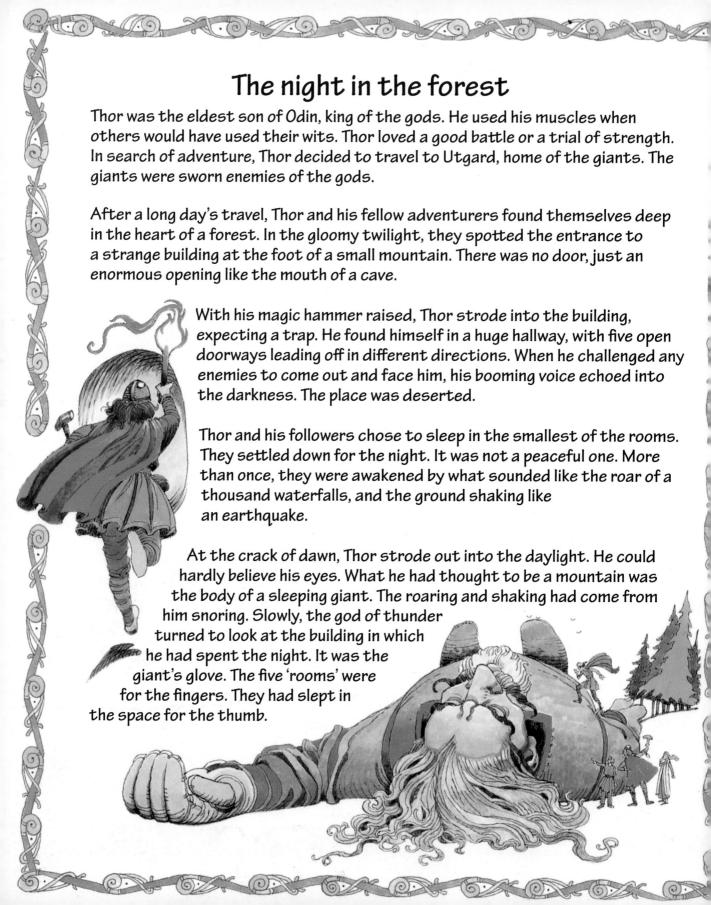

With his magic hammer raised, Thor strode into the building, expecting a trap. He found himself in a huge hallway, with five open doorways leading off in different directions. When he challenged any enemies to come out and face him, his booming voice echoed into the darkness. The place was deserted.

Thor and his followers chose to sleep in the smallest of the rooms. They settled down for the night. It was not a peaceful one. More than once, they were awakened by what sounded like the roar of a thousand waterfalls, and the ground shaking like an earthquake.

At the crack of dawn, Thor strode out into the daylight. He could hardly believe his eyes. What he had thought to be a mountain was the body of a sleeping giant. The roaring and shaking had come from him snoring. Slowly, the god of thunder turned to look at the building in which he had spent the night. It was the giant's glove. The five 'rooms' were for the fingers. They had slept in the space for the thumb.

Could the Vikings read and write?

Only a few of them could, but stories, like the one about Thor, were passed on by word of mouth from generation to generation. The parents told them to their children, and they told them to their children. Sagas weren't written down until the end of the Viking age.

The Viking alphabet was called the futhark, after the first six letters: f, u, th, a, r, k.

What was Viking writing like?

It was made up of 16 letters, or marks, called runes. They didn't have enough runes for every sound in the Viking language. This made spelling very difficult. Can you write your name in Viking runes?

These runes are carved on bone.

Reading from runes

| f | u | th | a | r | k | h | n | i | a | s | t | b | m | l | r |

So they didn't have books?

No, but they did have picture stones. These were usually gravestones, carved with pictures of great heroes and their adventures.

What did they write with?

Iron chisels and wooden mallets. They didn't have pens and paper. They cut letters into stone or wood, which was a pretty slow process. So writing was only used for really important things, like praising a great chief.

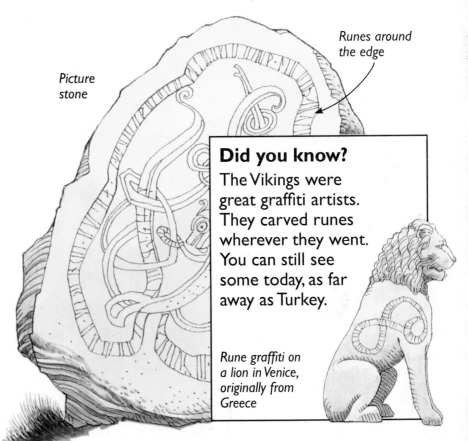

Picture stone

Runes around the edge

Did you know?

The Vikings were great graffiti artists. They carved runes wherever they went. You can still see some today, as far away as Turkey.

Rune graffiti on a lion in Venice, originally from Greece

How did the Vikings get around?

By ships and boats, mostly. The Viking lands were covered with mountains, fjords, rivers, lakes and islands. Vikings were all skilled sailors and shipbuilders. Thick forests provided plenty of wood for building boats.

Were there different types of boats?

Yes. Canoes, fishing boats, ferries, knorrs (trading ships) and, finest of all, the Viking warships. They were called longships, because they were so long, or dragon ships, because they had a dragon's head carved on the prow (front).

A knorr

A fishing boat

Dragon head

Prow

Cross beams and ribs helped strengthen the hull (the ship's body).

These people are building a longship.

Hitting the nail on the head

Tired boat-builder

Long planks of wood were very flexible in rough seas.

A picnic for the workers

Keel

Toolbox

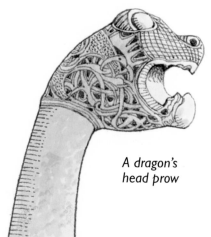

Why did the Vikings carve dragons' heads on their ships?

To scare their enemies, of course. It must have looked frightening to see a pair of wild eyes and snarling teeth **20** looming out of the fog.

A dragon's head prow

What was so special about longships?

They were so fast they cut through the water like knives. They were also very strong, but still light enough to be carried if necessary. They were also very shallow in the water.

You'll find he fell off his ladder on page 7, too.

Stern

Oars

Nailing a finger

Tar

Iron rivets

This holds up the mast and sail when they're not being used.

Why were their ships so shallow?

So they could sail quickly and quietly up shallow rivers. Even when the longships were packed with warriors, they could take a village completely by surprise.

Who built them, and how?

Professional ship-builders, but the whole village might join in. There was probably a shipyard attached to most big villages. The best ships were made of oak, but pine and birch were also used.

How did they travel in winter?

If the lakes and rivers were frozen over, people got around on skis, ice skates and horse-drawn sleighs. But they didn't travel much in winter.

How do we know about Viking ships?

Because some ships that were buried or sank at sea have survived, even though they are over a thousand years old. Sometimes even when the wood has rotted, the nails survive and we can make out the shape of the ship.

The remains of a Viking ship

21

Did the Vikings go shopping?

Not often. Most Vikings lived in the country and grew and made the things they needed for themselves. There were shops and markets in the towns, though. Merchants and craftspeople journeyed long distances to reach them.

What was it like in a Viking town?

Crowded and smoky from all the fires in people's houses. Most towns were by the sea, or on the edge of a river, so people could arrive by boat.

What kinds of crafts did people make?

Leatherworkers made shoes and boots. Bronze and silversmiths made necklaces, brooches and dishes. Bone carvers made pins and combs from deer antlers. Blacksmiths made tools and weapons.

  If you look very carefully, you can just about make out some of these people at work.

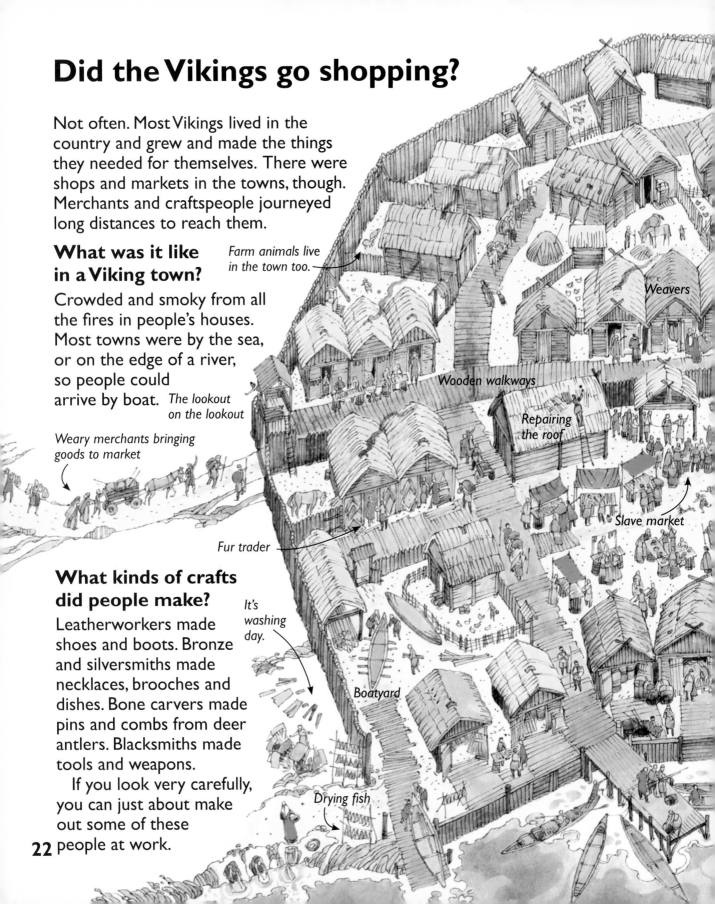

Farm animals live in the town too.

Weavers

Wooden walkways

The lookout on the lookout

Repairing the roof

Weary merchants bringing goods to market

Slave market

Fur trader

It's washing day.

Boatyard

Drying fish

22

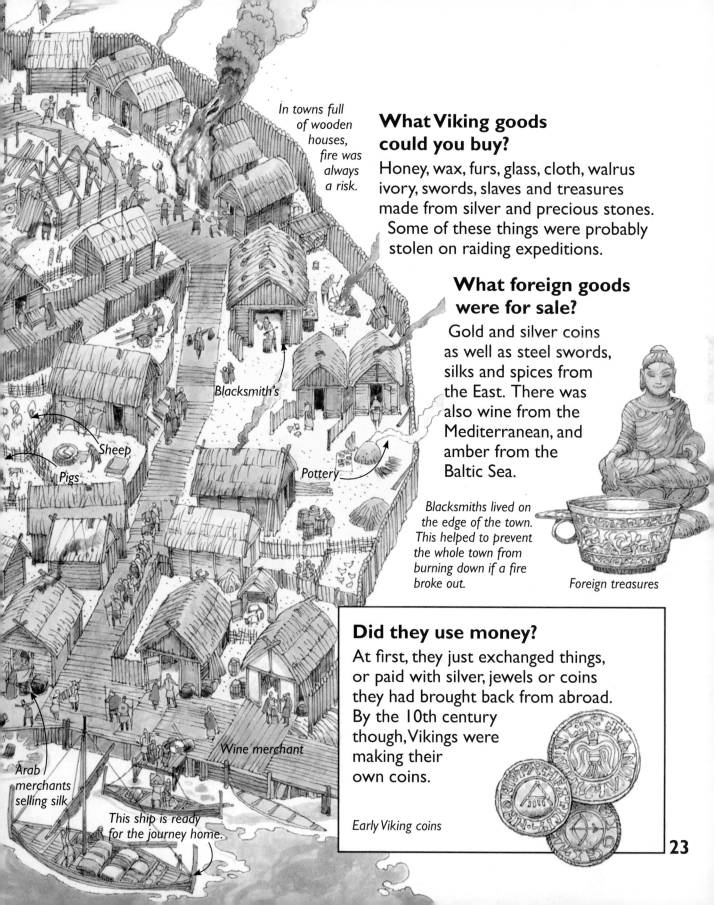

In towns full of wooden houses, fire was always a risk.

Blacksmith's

Sheep

Pigs

Pottery

Arab merchants selling silk

This ship is ready for the journey home.

Wine merchant

What Viking goods could you buy?

Honey, wax, furs, glass, cloth, walrus ivory, swords, slaves and treasures made from silver and precious stones. Some of these things were probably stolen on raiding expeditions.

What foreign goods were for sale?

Gold and silver coins as well as steel swords, silks and spices from the East. There was also wine from the Mediterranean, and amber from the Baltic Sea.

Blacksmiths lived on the edge of the town. This helped to prevent the whole town from burning down if a fire broke out.

Foreign treasures

Did they use money?

At first, they just exchanged things, or paid with silver, jewels or coins they had brought back from abroad. By the 10th century though, Vikings were making their own coins.

Early Viking coins

23

Did the Vikings have kings?

Yes, plenty of them. All at once. As time went on, there were fewer kings, but the ones that were left had more land and power. In the end, there were just three – one each for Denmark, Sweden and Norway.

How much power did the early kings have?

Probably not as much as they would have liked. But they were more important than the jarls and karls.

A king

A jarl

What were jarls?

The richest, most important chiefs. They owned lots of land and employed other Viking warriors.

Who were the karls?

Free men and women. Karls could fight and own their own land, and the men could vote at the Thing.

A karl

Wasn't everyone free?

The slaves, or thralls, weren't. They had a pretty tough time, working hard for no pay. Thralls could be bought and sold for a few furs or a barrel of wine.

24 *A thrall*

What's a Thing?

An open-air meeting, where Vikings met to discuss local problems, settle arguments and punish criminals. Things were held only every two or three years, but they lasted for days. People took them very seriously.

This thief has been sent away forever.

These women are enjoying a chat before supper.

His family is very sad to see him go.

This man is being tried for stealing horses.

These people are late. They were so busy raiding, they forgot about the Thing.

A thief hoping to steal a horse

Three chiefs have been chosen to act as judges.

A man called the lawspeaker recites the law to the crowd.

When the business is over, everyone enjoys themselves. These people are watching a horse-fight.

This quarrel is being settled by a duel.

How did they settle arguments?

Usually the judges decided who was in the right and who was in the wrong. But if they really couldn't make up their minds, they might try to ask the gods.

This man is being made to walk on hot stones. The Vikings believe that, if he is innocent, the gods will stop his feet burning. This is called "trial by ordeal".

What kinds of punishments did they have?

A criminal could be outlawed (sent away forever), fined, made a slave or, in extreme cases, put to death. Rich people got bigger fines.

Did they have an army?

Not exactly, but chiefs had bodyguards and all Viking men learned how to use weapons from an early age. They needed good fighting skills to be successful raiders. They also had to defend their homes and fight off pirates.

What weapons did they use?

Swords for stabbing people, and axes with huge blades for chopping people's heads off. They were very proud of their weapons, and even gave them names like *Skull-splitter*, *Leg-biter* and *The Adder*.

Wooden shield covered in leather

Padded leather jacket

Viking warriors ready for battle

This man's axe is called "Dragon-slayer".

Sword

What did they wear to protect themselves?

Not much. One very strange group of warriors, called the berserkers, even fought without any protection. People thought they must have magic powers. When the berserkers were around, everyone was scared – even other Vikings!

This shirt, made of thousands of iron rings, is called a byrnie. Most people can't afford this.

A brave priest

Weren't people frightened of them?

Yes, absolutely terrified. The Vikings were the most feared warriors of their time. People called them "the terror of the North".

This decorated sword probably belonged to a Viking chief.

This fine helmet is made of copper and leather. Notice that it doesn't have any horns or wings on it.

These people may be lucky enough to escape.

Where did they go raiding?
All over Europe – from Germany, Britain and Ireland, around the coasts of France and Spain as far as Italy.

These are the raiders who were late for the Thing on page 25.

A church was usually the best place to find treasure.

These women are going to be carried off as slaves.

Did they ride into battle?
Some of the chiefs did, but most warriors couldn't afford a horse. Instead they ran into battle, waving their weapons, and screaming at their terrified victims.

This woman knows how to use a broom.

Did you know?
Vikings sometimes buried their treasure in hoards. Archeologists have found so many of these, it looks as if some people forgot where they had buried things, or died before they could dig them up.

Decorated box found in a hoard

27

Were all Vikings ruthless raiders?

Not at all, but the raiders gave them a bad name. Viking merchants went abroad for trading, not raiding. Other Vikings went looking for a place to live.

SWEDEN

RUSSIA

Viking routes

Constantinople

Baghdad

MEDITERRANEAN SEA

Where did Viking traders go?

All over Europe, north and west to Iceland and Greenland, south down the Russian rivers as far as the rich city of Constantinople (now Istanbul in Turkey), and across deserts to the city of Baghdad (now in Iraq).

A small disagreement

This is a busy market in Constantinople

Drinks for thirsty shoppers

An Arab trader

Scales for weighing metals

This man is sure he is being cheated, but he isn't.

Unlucky slave girls for sale

A proud carpet seller from Persia

This man's customers have come all the way from China.

These men are bringing another log to the front of the boat.

Hauling the boat overland

Did they really go all that way by boat?

No. Some of the rivers had dangerous rapids, and some of the routes went overland. Then they had to carry their boats to the next river, by hauling them across the ground on logs.

Were the Vikings good craftsmen and women?

Yes, they made beautiful things, carved in wood, bone, gold and silver. Viking designs look like a lot of swirling lines. If you look closely, you can often see that these are really animals and monsters gripping on to each other.

This sort of design is known as a 'gripping beast'.

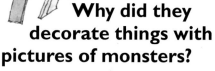

Decorated bronze part of a horse harness

Gold pendant

Silver brooch

Woodcarver at work

Why did they decorate things with pictures of monsters?

Because Vikings believed the seas and skies were full of them, often with magical powers. By carving monsters on things, they thought they could protect themselves from danger.

Sharp swords and knives from France

Did you know?

Russia is actually named after a Viking tribe called the Rus. This is because the first ever kingdom in Russia was set up in the 9th century by a Rus man called Rurik.

Russian style Viking silver

How far did Viking settlers go?

A long way. There were Viking settlements in Russia, France, Britain, Ireland, Iceland, Greenland and even North America.

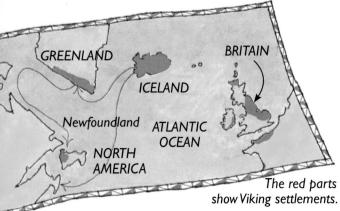

The red parts show Viking settlements.

GREENLAND

BRITAIN

ICELAND

Newfoundland

ATLANTIC OCEAN

NORTH AMERICA

What was it like on board ship?

Cold, wet and very uncomfortable. In a storm it would have been pretty frightening too. Crossing the ocean was much slower in those days.

How did they find their way?

With difficulty. Although they had years of experience, they had no instruments to guide them – only the sun and stars. Sometimes they followed flocks of birds and shoals of fish.

Amazing Viking bird monster

Seabirds flying south for winter

Beards flying in the wind

Barrels of food and drink for the trip

This chicken has had enough.

Camping things

Fresh water

Sea water

The type of boat is called a knorr. It is wider, deeper and slower than a longship.

Did you know?

The picture on the left is of a bronze weather vane from a Viking ship. Streamers would be attached to the tiny holes along the bottom. These would rattle and blow in the wind, showing the sailors where the wind was coming from.

30

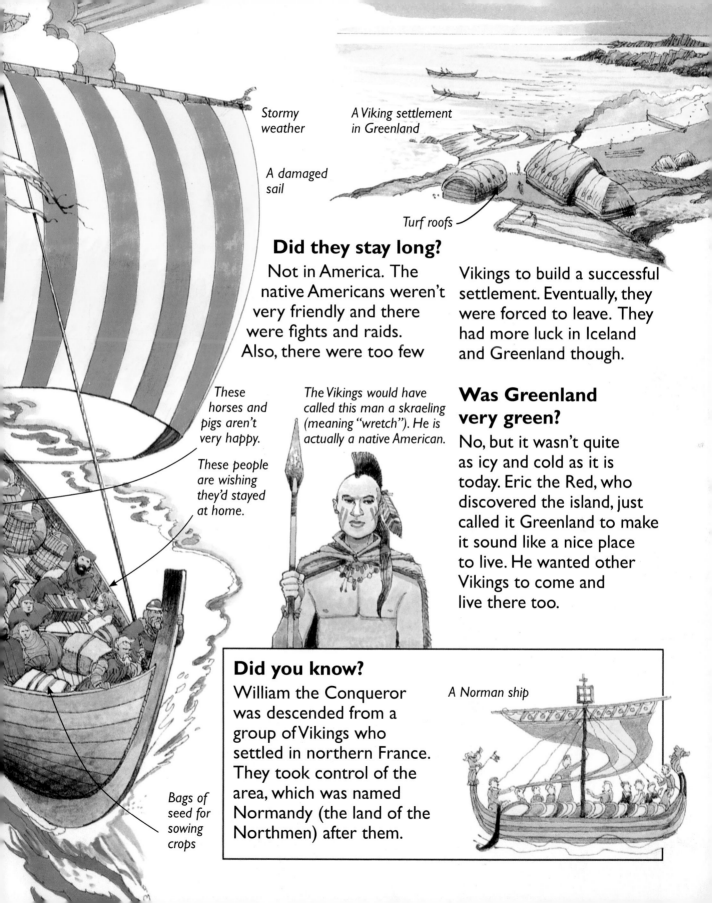

Stormy weather

A Viking settlement in Greenland

A damaged sail

Turf roofs

Did they stay long?

Not in America. The native Americans weren't very friendly and there were fights and raids. Also, there were too few Vikings to build a successful settlement. Eventually, they were forced to leave. They had more luck in Iceland and Greenland though.

These horses and pigs aren't very happy.

These people are wishing they'd stayed at home.

The Vikings would have called this man a skraeling (meaning "wretch"). He is actually a native American.

Was Greenland very green?

No, but it wasn't quite as icy and cold as it is today. Eric the Red, who discovered the island, just called it Greenland to make it sound like a nice place to live. He wanted other Vikings to come and live there too.

Bags of seed for sowing crops

Did you know?

William the Conqueror was descended from a group of Vikings who settled in northern France. They took control of the area, which was named Normandy (the land of the Northmen) after them.

A Norman ship

Index

America, 2, 30, 31
amulets, 11
archeologists, 3, 14, 27
Asgard, 10, 11

berserkers, 26
Bifrost, 10, 11
Britain, 2, 27, 30
Byzantine Empire, 3

chess, 17
children, 6, 9
clothes, 4, 9
Constantinople, 3, 28
craftspeople, 2, 22, 29

Denmark, 2, 3, 24
dwarfs, 10

elves, 10, 11
Ericsson, Leif, 2
Eric the Red, 2, 31

farms, 2, 6
flax, 4
food, 7, 12, 14-15, 30
France, 2, 27, 30, 31
furniture, 9
futhark, 19

giants, 10, 11, 18
gods and goddesses, 10-11,
    13, 17, 25
graffiti, 19
graves, 12, 13, 14
Greenland, 2, 8, 28, 30, 31

hairstyles, 5
helmets, 4, 26
hnefatfl, 17

32 Iceland, 2, 28, 30, 31

Iraq, 3, 28
Ireland, 2, 30

jarls, 24
jewels, 5, 23, 29

karls, 24
kings, 3, 24

magic, 11, 12, 26, 29
medicine, 12
Middle East, 2, 17
Midgard, 10, 11
money, 23
monsters, 10, 29, 30
music, 14, 15

Newfoundland, 30
Niflheim, 11, 13
Normandy, 2, 31
Norse language, 3
Northmen, 2, 31
Norway, 2, 3, 24
Novgorod, 3

Odin, 10

parties, 14, 15, 16

raiders, 2, 3, 25, 26, 27, 28
runes, 19
Rurik, 29
Russia, 3, 4, 28, 29, 30

sagas, 17, 19
ships, 20-21, 28, 30, 31
    knorrs, 20, 30
    longships, 3, 20-21
    ship burials, 12, 13, 21
skalds, 14, 15
slaves, 6, 13, 23, 24, 25, 27
Sweden, 2, 3, 24, 28

Things (meetings), 24-25, 27
Thor, 10, 11, 17, 18
thralls, 24 (also see slaves)
toilets, 9
towns, 22-23
traders, 2, 17, 18
treasure, 2, 13, 23, 27
Turkey, 19, 28

Utgard, 18

Valhalla, 12, 13
Valkyries, 13
Varangian guard, 3

warriors, 2, 12, 21, 26, 27
weapons, 12, 13, 22, 26, 27
writing, 19

Yggdrasil, 10

Answers
Page 5
*The items are:
a key, a needle and a
pair of tweezers.*

This edition first published in 2015 by
Usborne Publishing Ltd, 83-35 Saffron Hill,
London EC1N 8RT, England.
www.usborne.com

Copyright © 2015, 1995 Usborne Publishing
Ltd. The name Usborne and the devices
are Trade Marks of Usborne
Publishing Ltd.